Under My Hood

Ron Benson
Lynn Bryan
Kim Newlove
Liz Stenson
Iris Zammit

CONSULTANTS
Florence Brown
Estella Clayton
Susan Elliott-Johns
Charolette Player
Shari Schwartz
Lynn Swanson
Helen Tomassini
Debbie Toope

Prentice Hall Ginn

Contents

Popcorn   **3**
personal recount by
Liz Stenson

My Weather Diary   **8**
personal diary by
Iris Zammit

Winter Clothes   **15**
poem by Karla Kuskin

Weather Questions   **21**
question/answer report
by Shari Schwartz
and Helen Tomassini

Ricardo's Writing
question/answer report

Popcorn

by Liz Stenson
Illustrated by Isabel Langevin

When winter snow lay on the ground, we picked out seeds for our garden.

I picked out popcorn seeds.

When spring rain fell on the ground, we planted the seeds.

I planted the popcorn seeds.

When summer sun warmed the ground, we watered the plants.

I watered the popcorn plants.

When fall leaves lay on the ground, we picked the vegetables.

I picked the popcorn.

When snow lay on the ground again, we popped the popcorn.

I ate the popcorn!

My Weather Diary

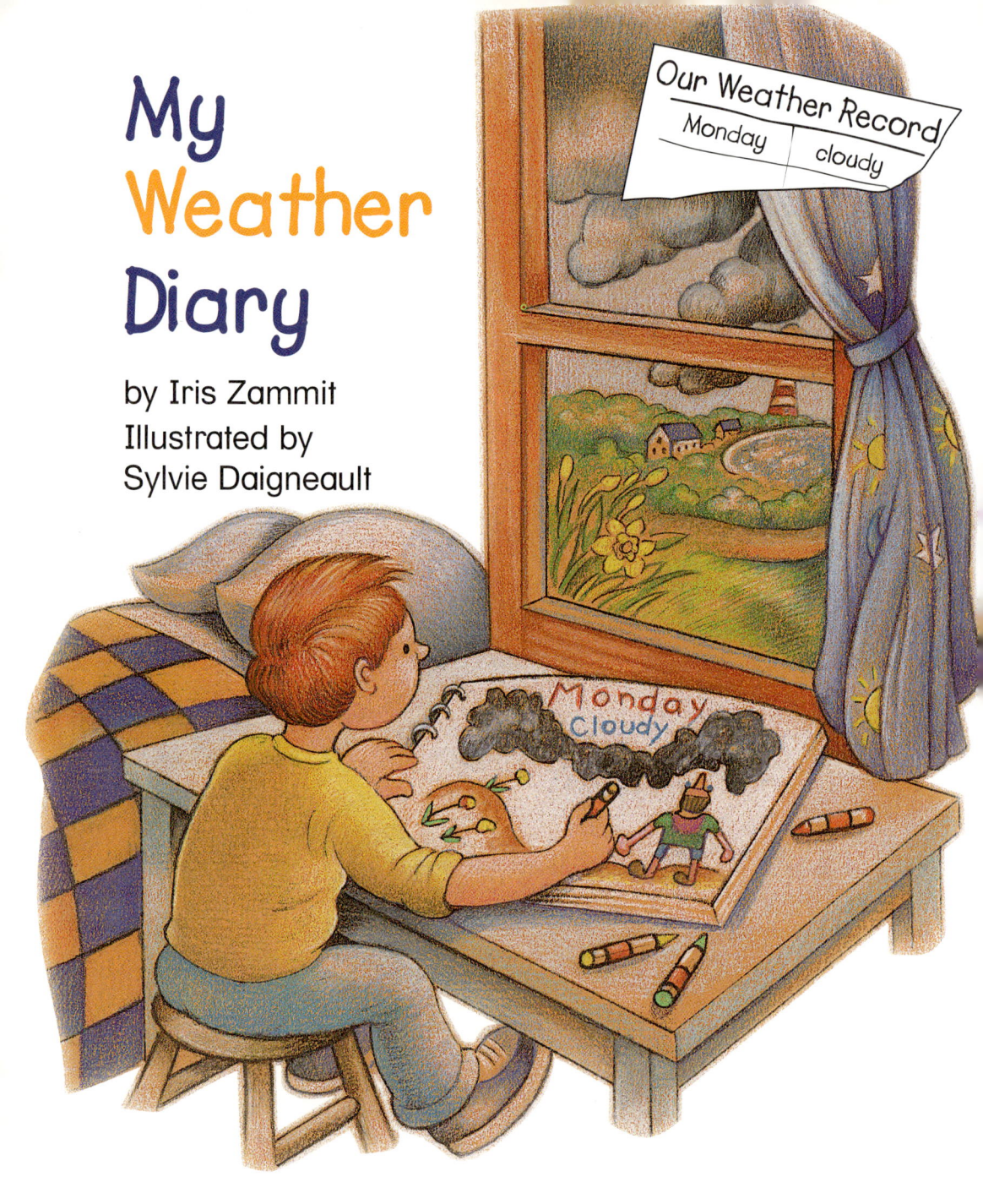

by Iris Zammit
Illustrated by Sylvie Daigneault

Monday was a cloudy day.
I smelled rain in the air.

Tuesday was a foggy day.
I heard the foghorn on the bay.

Wednesday was a chilly day.
I made hot chocolate. Yummy!

Thursday was a stormy day.
I saw lightning zigzag
across the sky.

Friday was a rainy day.
I felt raindrops on my nose.

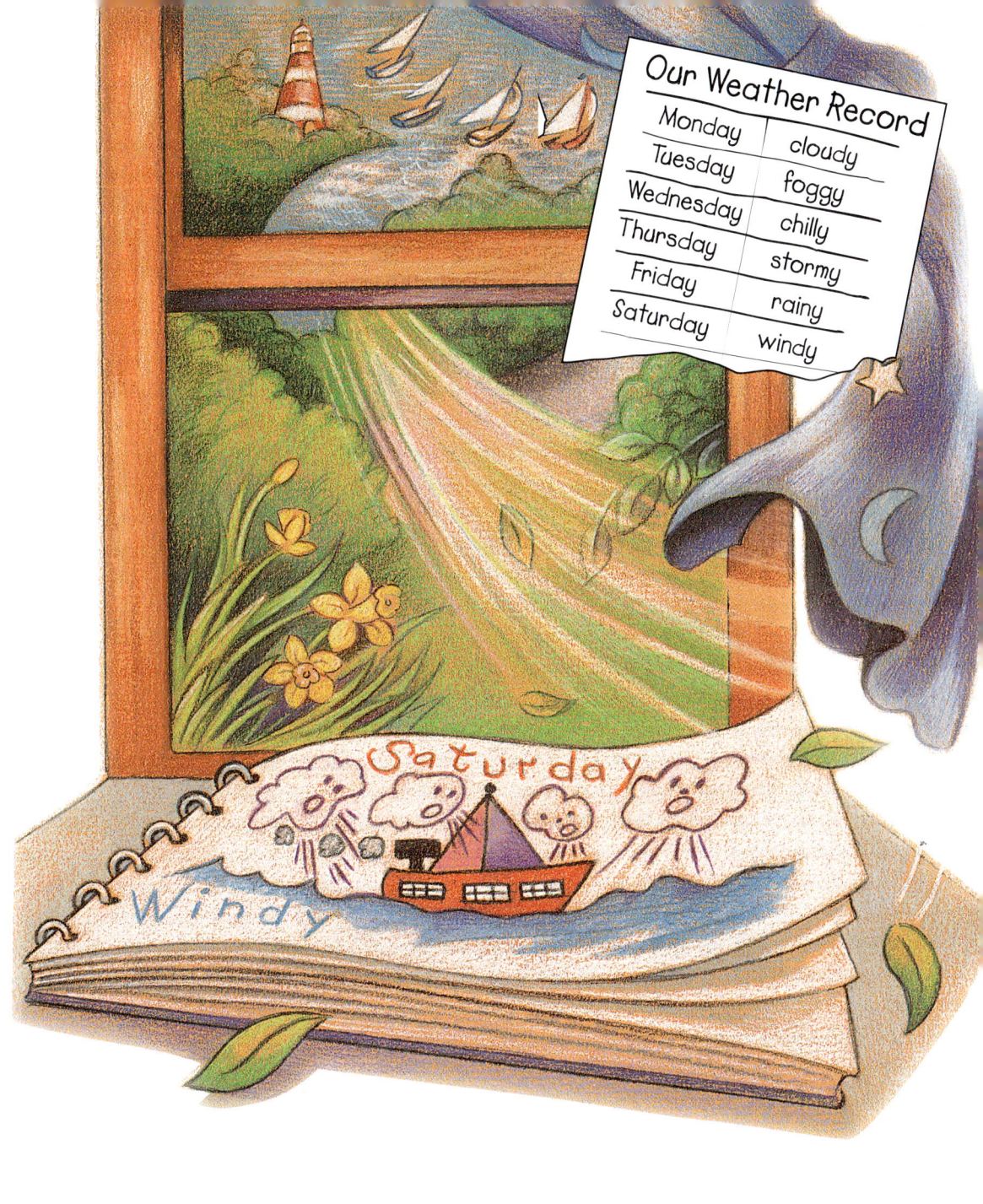

Saturday was a windy day.
I saw sailboats on the water.

Our Weather Record	
Monday	cloudy
Tuesday	foggy
Wednesday	chilly
Thursday	stormy
Friday	rainy
Saturday	windy
Sunday	sunny

Sunday was a sunny day.
I think that's why it's called Sunday.

Winter Clothes

by Karla Kuskin
Illustrated by Laurie Stein

Under my hood I have a hat
And under that
My hair is flat.

Under my coat
My sweater's blue.
My sweater's red.
I'm wearing two.

My muffler muffles to my chin
And round my neck
And then tucks in.

My gloves were knitted
By my aunts.
I've mittens too
And pants

And pants
And boots
And shoes
With socks inside.
The boots are rubber,
red and wide.

And when I walk
I must not fall
Because I can't get up at all.

Weather Questions

by Shari Schwartz and Helen Tomassini

How are clouds made?

Clouds are made when lots of water drops and dust stick together.

What is fog?

Fog is a cloud that is close to the ground.

Why does rain fall?

Rain falls because the water drops in the cloud get too big and heavy.

Why are there rainbows?

There are rainbows because the sunlight shines through drops of water.